Spiderwize
Remus House
Coltsfoot Drive
Woodston
Peterborough
PE2 9BF

www.spiderwize.com

MUSTARD CHILDREN

DANICA TRIM

Contents

For R,
who passed by...

Anniversaries

Anniversaries
Take note -
These notches do
Bear witness
To change
And changelessness.

The newfangled
And the old designs
Creep in
Side by side
And wait to be remembered
Now and then

These days
Are reflections
Held this way and that
Below an arc of dust
And we say

"Here we are,"
We know how we travelled -
Seeing and not seeing
All things marked,
We look forward
To the arrival.

Time

Given hands that spin
We are all given in,
Handed over at last
Wisely turning over the past
Stroked by the universal

No more, no longer swinging the lead,
Bring out, bring out, bring out your dead
Per capita, proceeds the pendulum
And closes each compendium.

Memento mori, darling,
Find your modus vivendi;
Tête à têtes and billets doux,
All the things you send me
Inside I will accrue
All parts of you.

Temper, temper,
Amor semper,
The wheel unwinds -
We never have been bound
But in the round

Time will come and yes the father will
Take it all, body, mind and painted face
Put up the shelf and make a space –
Remember me, remember me.

Playtime

Falling down, never
Through the hoop
Slips effortlessly into a new group
Sliding and smiling,
They whip her away,
Skipping fantastical favours today.

Delving in holes, dug out
Pins and needles from the squatting and kneeling,
Pain from a graze,
Pictures of rain
Don't look like the sky now.

Running round looking -
Am I late?
I'm chasing a wild thing so class can wait;
Choosing and shaping
My own new device,
I wonder if grown-ups are just as nice.

Living at Home

I do not belong to this room;
It was my doing
Because I came back
When things weren't right,
Or never left
The window is the same one
I left behind
Open in summer
And even a little ajar in winter
Where the air grows slippery against the panes

I could find my way round in the dark;
No stumbling blocks,
Except the ones I always found
Nothing comes close -
I am not on my own.

This is not really my place;
Better than nowhere
Much better
No one's been in touch
From the old days,
Though they might do;
It's an old and new space

Nevertheless
I do not belong to this room;
I stay here
Till it's time to go out
Or someone calls at the door.

Bathroom Cabinet

Tubes and tubes of things unused,
Ancient unguents escaped and oozed;
Plasters in packets now battered with age,
Hair gel arrived at the concreted stage;
Wax bought to aid DIY depilation,
Discarded because of some new innovation.

Liniments garnered to deal with our strains,
Cheap aspirins to take away pains;
Antihistamines sort out the summer hay fever,
Anti depressants, another reliever.

Blister packs popped till there's only one pill,
Toothpaste and toothpicks and mouthwash to swill;
Aftersun smelling of holiday nights,
Creams that will soothe our red rashes and bites.

One day I must tidy this collection I've built,
Replace all the products whose contents have spilt;
Then check my reflection still merits a pass,
So I don't find I'm also replacing the glass.

Need

This grows from me like
A thing uncalled for
Like a hair from a part of me
Which should be bald -
I will have to pluck it out.

This gives me pain like
When my stomach's sore
Like an after dinner ache I
Can't sit and smile -
I will have to take a pill.

This makes me itch like
An all over rash
Like something calling for my nails
To scratch it out -
I will have to calm it down.

Now I shudder
Wanting to turn away;
I want to want an emetic
But I need to swallow,
Need to take it in;
Something genetic
Leads me to follow
And I must accede,
There is no anaesthetic
But I'll be numb enough one day
So there's no need.

Lost

The joys of blue pills
And blue carpets
Getting lost,
Popped out
Into a colour the same,
Not even a crinkle's difference
Glances
Sweeping the floor
Leave the cure
Behind, unseen,
Unknown in the frame
Of the door.

Two Labs

New life in a dish
That wasn't supposed to happen,
But fulfils a couple's wish.

Being inventive
With a view to power saving,
A measure that's preventive.

No hurry for either endeavour;
We are only allowed to be so clever.

River

This song is a river
And runs through hills
Where I expect the melody to go
It turns up and down and on
Words come and flow
And I don't know
When they ebb and slow.

This song is a river
And makes its way
By itself and I can only follow
Its direction surprising
My level low
It cannot grow
Within a stone's throw.

This song is a river,
It used to wriggle from me
Like a sour stream
Now wide, it gets away from me
Beside what goes on in banks
And pours dreams
I cannot stop and see
One day I will sail on the song
Before it bursts and I lose my key.

Explorers

I will take you to the bottom of the ocean;
Rich, jewelled and gleaming
Lies a wreck
In our search lights,
And if we were dreaming
We could see the dancing
Death in motion,
Walking on the deck
A thousand, thousand nights.

They do not know what passes in the world above
For life and its leisures.
Nothing stirs
But wraiths in rooms
Indulging their pleasures
Awash with years the same -
What could they love?
Greedy Neptune purrs;
A deeper sleeper looms.

Come with me to dance beneath broken chandeliers,
Oblivious to woe
Smiles are high;
Fish cannot reach
The pearlescent new glow
Where it does not belong.
No salty tears
From a living eye
Can fall or fill the breach.

In Your Shoes

A little fey,
Funny and full of it
Shrinking from flowery faffing,
You were the girl who half wanted
To be a boy,
But you had to let
Your femininity shine through
So you chose a flat shoe in
Pink, whereas
Little Boy Blue
Couldn't bear the stink
Of locker rooms and
Boasts of birds and
Bloody awright mate
How's it going, mate
Slap on the back
Pat on the back
Did you have her?
Good on yer, mate
Blokedom, but
He still showed off
And never mentioned
Ballet
To the football studs.

He Guards Against The Seeker

Does she know where the treasures are hidden?
He wonders if she saw the chest in the cave
And if she plans to stage a raid.
Overstepping the mark is forbidden,
She should know it's reserved for only the brave
And mind the traps that he has laid.

Does she know all the measures he's taken?
He thinks she may see the armour is hollow,
Press forth and seize what he holds dear.
He will hold out, for she is mistaken,
Though she must have a plan she plans to follow -
But best laid plans remain unclear.

Does she know all the pleasures of hunting?
He likes to keep trophies, not only his own;
She must not stray and see his hoard.
Does she know what it is she's confronting?
Why must she keep coming, till cover is blown?
He does not want to be explored.

Does she know he is really a good one?
One forced in his course to resort to deceit;
He doesn't see why he should share.
Guarding what's his against any or none,
He hopes she will tire soon and make her retreat.
He'll wait a while, then clear the air.

Snake

No flat foot dancer he -
The being that time begot
Winds one trail, faint
And knows not sleight of hand.
He tails bigger flesh
That went before and will come after
Eyes that do not scorn
And do not know love, laughter,
Only how to draw in
The sand
This, he has not forgot

No light deviation -
Time gives focus on hard ground,
Myth swept clean, stark -
A memory mistook.
Instinct will not balk;
It seeks and pins the object desired
Fills the tasteless maw
With a new subject, inspired
Nowhere near the fall
His book
Left, only prey word bound

No single simple skein -
Unravelling his full form
Tips the scales, knots
Unwinding framed fury.
A blinding flash struck,
Vanished is the fight and calm abounds.
Nothing more is known -
Intent unfelt sits, and wounds,
No will yet suborned,
Jury
Out, condemns the dull worm.

Mengkak Links

I have an attachment to chickens;
They were colourful in the longhouse yard, and loud
Without too much of an audience,
And pale and dull
In shrink wrap when they were chilling,
Surrounded by the crowds.

I have an attachment to dogs;
They were beckoning in the longhouse yard, alert,
With a few chickens their audience,
And thin but full
They mingled with tomorrow's meal –
Guardians, not dessert.

Some time since then
A dragon forced its way
Into the yard
With a tube and flashing colours
And sounds from the world
To which we now have an attachment.
It is granting an audience
And we lap around its mouth
Waiting for words and pictures
To come out.

Dog's Life

No time like the present,
No time at all,
Only now the brown eyed stare
And the wordless question
Touch me, care for me, give me meat.
I love you,
But I don't know what forever means,
So I can't make promises
Without premise;
Only now I need your warm floor,
Cushioned gaze and sweet affection.
There is no shall or will or hope,
Just the certainty
I will remember
If you hurt me.

One Love

One for the master
One for the road
One to go faster
One to download

One for the night time
One for the day
One careful white line
One all the way

One for the sunshine
One for the storm
One for a fun time
One's just the norm

One for the bedpost
One for the boys
One for the west coast
One for my joys

One for the songbird
One little hook
One is the wrong word
One for the book

One for the hero
One for a dame
One more than zero
One of the same

Soliloquy in a Bookshop

Among the stories
He spoke and never looked up,
Uttered loudly
And scolded his own outburst.
Utterly
Mad? I don't know
Because we all wait
For others to tell us so.
He was an island
In a sea of books
Who could afford to ignore
The looks
And store his own security,
Self contained
He leaves
But not before
The last admonishment -
Stop.
Repeat the words
"You'd better not"
Be glib and glad of what you've got.

Words

Words
Formless things
On their own I
Suppose
In a pool
Without limbs
They can't climb
Without

You

Find
A stick, that's
The thing to do
Something
Buoyant to
Break surface
Rise above
The ordinary

We

Do
Try so hard
Leaving body
Pieces
In the banks
Strewn around
To be found
Out.

Gentle as hell.

Muse

If I were a man
I would go for you
Because you are not
The most beautiful in the room.
Ah, what is beauty after all
That glossy, blank, unused
Frontispiece which foretells little
And hides nothing, so plain,
So that, grown old, it is only dull
And has only lost, not gained?

But you have paragraphs
Behind your eyes
And narratives jump from between
The lines that form whenever you laugh
And your plots are never expected,
So I, if I were a man,
Would be suspended
From your every word.

I do not admire in the same way,
But I do aspire to get under your skin
Other than a man does,
Gently brushing off the covers,
To be like you, liked by you,
Gifted with that dust called magic.

Fear

Fear is strange ground
Sometimes crowded by a herd,
Sometimes the rich soil of solitude,
The soul of the absurd
Which can constantly confound

Laughter halts all
Sometimes spouting ridicule,
Sometimes the spoil of inaptitude,
The spell of the dark fool
Menaces and overrules

Facing lions
Sometimes roaring in defence,
Sometimes the foil of fortitude,
The fall of good sense
Dashed away when called upon

This sense demands defiance
Commands compliance
Gives defendant valour
To the aggressor
Wins or loses wars
According not unto itself
But only caprice -
So why bother?

Jerusalem

You will not find an old city sleeping
But sometimes, dormant, like the truth, it lies
And faces brown and lined
With ground in dirt of ages
You will find seeking;
But no weeping
For each inch and etch that age has wrought
And brought down towers and walls to ruin and memory;
What heaven built man's soul destroys -
In carnal grist is rent and borrowed
Back for stories now and then
Thrown up, applauded, and the curtain then drawn down
The next endless act will follow
Words given up for dust,
But light never fully dawns
For prayers are said and answered briefly,
Lashes hanging, still half used
In quartered light, the old city breathes and muses
On its unforgotten soul.

Politics

Ah, an indiscretion -
How charming!
You could write it on the street;
If you do it well
Others will find it
Quite disarming.
Oh how neat!
We all need something for our meat.

Exposure

There was a time
When I
Was like a timid vole -
Underscoring all my weaknesses
Was a tendency to climb into a hole.

Today's the day
When I
Shall swoop to the entrance
And finding myself there shall plunge in
To eat the bitter part of my little heart,
Leaving nothing to chance

Tomorrow goes
When I
No longer find this shape
In favour and cannot fly or hide
So air is cut away from wings and bright eyes;
This is almost escape
And leaves the world open wide.

Martyr

For you, for love,
Forbidden, forgiven,
I give this day to night
And choose flight, though it does not stay my fight
For this I know –
Experience is sweet
Before it deals a blow;
So crowned like a coloured deity
I am smashed before the laity.
Belief is gone, and theists thickly mutter
My prayers are up to the ceiling,
My books are cut about,
And feeble eyelids flutter.

But for you, for love,
Comes now the noblest part,
Never mind, but humbly,
The burning of my heart.

Rose

A depth of roses,
Garden dropped head thick with perfumed lucre
Rich without borders
Thousands range wide
Nightly warming a glowing shell in bed.
This is a darkening.

Bring it into a room -
Just one, no need for a hot house;
Multitudes can mix
And frankincense can touch the petalled edges
Ever, ever proclaiming the smell of God.

The tea we drink
Is mollified by milk
Yet somewhere within the scent of foreign
Steam clouds echo
Rose words and dust leaves
Burning from ground
To firmament.

Heart

Symbol of love
Because you are reckless
How is it that you keep the beat
Blazoned on an arm
Red rests
Thrown out,
Not so keen
On the mind,
For she is not daft
And dies nothing unexpected?

Hope sewn into your jacket,
Pocketed lazily like a watch
Offering understanding,
Never had the time
Even when you asked.
Deep in my bowels
I feel the burn of analysis;
Everything's on the turn now.

Under attack
A figurative sense
Felt between the stars and the dark
Moon had a sister
Blue blood
Pumped out
Forever
Love blinded
The sun shines and fades
And does nothing unexpected.

First Love

I remember summer half a lifetime ago,
When in half light I was touched by the moon and you,
And outside you could clearly hear
The birds proclaiming
This was something new.

I remember the texture of wood
And climbing over fences,
Just the two of us spending everything
Because it was secret and because it was good.

I remember morning had broken over us,
When the mystery had gone and I had woken;
I didn't know this was just a
Bead along the string –
Add here, a token.

I remember the heat of days out
And warm kisses on the stairs;
Only pretty lances pricked our pleasure -
Sweetly majestic morning suns do not blaze doubt.

I remember a night in a pale blue nimbus,
When all that passed is clouded in a rosy hue;
I understood your right hand had
Reached to breach the bank –
I was changed by you.

I remember wide eyes seeking stars
And the premise of two halves;
Many feelings, though never this again
Come past the blinds, the beaded string, and rattle bars.

Fire Works

The boys have made fire today,
Just a little glow
In a
Wild meadow,
Vivid, wanders wide across the colour wheel
A waving ocean crossing vessel.

The boys played with fire today,
Intemperate haste
With a
Wild foretaste,
Fervid, teases tongues past skin too flushed to feel
A cooling ebb and flow essential.

The boys quenched a fire today,
No wild abandon
But their
Mild hands on,
Placid, eased the embers to a waxen seal
Locked down in smoking glassy entrails.

The boys laid a fire today,
Fallen old wood sticks
And a
Wild phoenix,
Arid, dusty dry from ancient ashes steal
And fade to grey before renewal.

Wood

Gold box
Match edged with a token from you,
Wood light in early Autumn,
This is the place
We came to sin.
Goodly looked the sun upon us
On that day

Gold leaf
Caught just beyond life on your head
Hinge snapped just before you came,
The only place
You sighed at last,
Gently creaked the lid you laid on
Just for me.

Gold edged
Black painted scenes well imagined
Trees, spread with us at their heels.
This is the place
For everything
Simply fitted, blown by your breath,
Made for me.

Piece

Stroke by stroke
On a blank canvas
I made you till I
Could plough your ridges
And dance even when I was afraid
In your farmyard

Frame by frame
Shutters blink candour,
I made this sitting;
No smile tells it all
And I always want to make a stand
In your long room

Pace by piece,
Blanket canopy
I made you hover
Over my eye roam
And reflect all my own perspectives
In your sky parts.

Paper Trail

One day I shall have
Read more books
Than I've seen trees.

I try to limit
Expectations
As there are far too many grasses to pick
And I am too illiberal
To assume bonuses and options
Even when the sun is shining

Up in the roof
There will be cobwebs
That will outlast me.

So many paths
To good intentions -
More like ladders
They need to be braced
Against a wall
For insurance
And mounted by only the brave.

Script

Anyone can do it now
And you'd let them, too,
Their digits all over everything
Round columns and keys
Address you in a feminine typeface
Conforming through thick and thin
Phrases shaped and honed
Good enough for monuments

Don't know if you're
About:blank
All clear, sentenced to nothing

In the lines of letters
Tiny bits of web
Counted in shorthand

Read the script, it's an invitation;
Judge all you want in the near beckoning,
Always aware, mind,
You may be a typographical error.

The Caller

He was talking to me,
I didn't understand his dialect
Well, what can you expect?
I've been out of it for so long.
He didn't understand me
Though why should he?
It's just what goes between us that goes wrong.

Apparently, I was
Supposed to get the nuances and nods
But I just felt at odds
With the structure of this old game.
He didn't get me at all;
Made his next call
To one who knows and lies but makes no claim.

Politics II

I will shoot my rhetoric
To stem your mutiny as ever
Across the bows,
The great divide -
Only for a second
I want to wring your neck
Yet shall refrain as
The ligature to me
Would more injurious be.
Smile, talk, laugh, walk,
Give hints and never break;
I shall be smooth as silk
And slip you with my warp and weft
And deftly cast you off, cut you out,
And it will be too late when you notice.
Your trouble is that you snap -
Not a willow, more a roughshod rider or a bull in china
Losing friends like leaves while others jump away;
I float, my sail shining white,
Smoothing over all
So prevailing winds will favour me,
I will smile, talk, laugh, walk,
And bury you at sea.

Our War

No idea what it was like:
Blood, cold, mud, bold, brown
Lions in heat;
A moment of hate
Is like a moment of ecstasy
Refracted in a filthy puddle
And you're up to your neck in it,
Blood dancing before you fall.

No idea at all, yet
I recall your face
All cheek, rushing red with blushes
When first we met
And grimaces of joy
Like a beast, not a boy,
We were together
Full of it, full of it,
A life of love
Over and over
Till you left and went
Up the line

Oh my Love
I will keep you alive,
I want no peace
To know I'm free;
If you pay
All the roar
Will end and
Silence will fall.

In this silence
The only sound is me.

Dumb

She made it nice
He made it too
Neither of them knew what to do
But they both smiled
To be among the few.
They love their little honey buns -
He said, she said,
Nice tits, nice guns.

Daily Beloved

Daily beloved, we are gathered here
In the sight of one another
To witness the dear departed,
Either loneliness or freedom
Severed by a lover.

With this ring all my worldly ways
Become yours and no more a lone traveller will I be
In sickness and in health
Forever cherished, free and not free.

We will spend some time
Touching each other with the
Exaggerated care taken of something newly got
That fades with familiarity,
So that later damage to the object
Matters not.

There is contempt in silence,
Just as much of it in love;
How can you tell the difference?

Daily beloved, we come together,
Had and held till death do us part,
Forsaking all other options,
Making vows that make off with all
The secrets of our hearts.

For R

You should have come from another era,
From the diplomatic corps,
British of course,
Tight lipped, open minded;
Should have been brought in
Over tea
Some kind of dance
Would be in order
Before climbing the back stairs,
Careful of creaking,
Working through the layers,
A coloured cupcake
Decrowned to dusty sponge;
An afternoon with you
Is like a rationing.

Icy eyes
I can feel you coming back
Unwanted, like an unwashed teacup,
Roses on china, gold rimmed
Brown inside
Always so
Careful of speaking
Just so
I am the tea girl
And I can have your golden smile
And polite twinkles
Across the white table
And your cake crumbs
Under it, if I like.

Would you like a silver spoon, sir?
Better than a shovel,
A dainty stuffing,
Better than a hole in a hovel.
Vanilla tones spout
Good things and great sorts,
And all I see is soiled starch
And a passing by.

Mustard Children

You and I
Would have mustard children:
Seed and sauce;
Grim spice awaits pretty girls,
Brown eyed boys egged on by simple things,
Paste clinging to goose pimples,
Young lives on course,
Earth colours their natural base,
Fired on the outside,
Yellow waving just beneath their faces.

You and I
Would have mustard children:
Pound for pound,
Too much and never enough,
Water on weak powder makes strong stuff,
Laced roughly doesn't take long.
Such a taste found,
Air hovers, waiting to return,
Cowered on the inside,
Not afraid to open a mouth that burns.

This is only speculation
And we are mixed
In our contempt of that.
Overriding all sense of taste,
Roughshod, bold, irritant, proud,
Lazy additives,
Our children would be mustard children:
Merry seedlings of truth met at a trading post,
All burnt minds and chicken thighs.

Fat and Sugar

He was ripe and she was plain,
She dry and he sweaty against the grain;
He folded her in as she scattered across his wet glistening...
Was someone listening?
Could they hear the mixing and spooning?
The fingering, rubbing, the kneading
Ballooning
The state they are now in forever
Blended, he'd hoped they might be raised together...

It was hot at the finish
Smelled of satisfaction,
Sweet, savoury edge
Of chemical reaction,
But the air cooled the mound
To the crust of disgust.

...he was ripe and she was plain,
Came out of the pipe, all glazed in vain.

Massage

Heavy fingertips
Alight and faint music streams
Ripple into open ears
While eyes are closed

Each knot is pushed out
Like a tendril
Worked through like an old tangled tale,
Yarn spun,
Teased apart

It is hard to take
Necessary pressure
To work it all out
Takes courage and strength.

I have never felt better;
Wish I could do this to myself,
Unwind gently,
And pull myself together.

Sleep

Sleep, you tiresome wanderer,
You make me withered
Where you wend your way and tread,
Lean against my shutters,
Lay your head,
Make me your bed,
Urging leave-taking by wakefulness
In dreary susurration
Hours are spent
In your wasteland
And, as if in spite,
You offer
Only dreamed landscapes
For your board.

Sleep, you eye hungry time pedlar,
You cart me off
And never settle down,
Except one day you will take me and
Leave me cold
For someone else
With warmer ways.

Still, I cannot resist you
Make my mind flutter,
Weight my head,
Send me nightly midwinter,
Toss away your leaves you left
And eventually I will see you
As you really are.

Briar Rose

I fear that I shall need the thorn
To prick me that I once was born
From nothing sprung, I cannot say
I leapt in joy to wake this way.

I did not dream - I knew not how
No peace felt yet no furrowed brow
My breath removed, I can't resist
An open kiss, the catalyst.

Danae

Shafted by the light
Clever golden guise
Lap God
Cast adrift, in a role of production,
Yellow pilot didn't have a voice
But he drove her there.

One king for another king,
Silver fish rock me
In this chest lies my way
Soft, downy one today,
Tomorrow's killer
My shield, my cause, my own being
Stripped away.

I know not if I am blessed.
I am merely shaped.

Angles

No more weakness -
Beneath damp sky
A winter day
We are
Straightforward as Teuton edged tongues we have,
We now plough through the streets
In metal shod.

As we cross
We look for vigilance, forward,
For a care;
There must be more to life than
Magpies and black cats.

Apply Tim and The Elfman

Hobby horse no legs
Big eyes wonder why
Wounds don't die;
Salve, here,
Apply, apply
My child,
Hello, world of love.

He looked in terrible wonder
At the flamingo
And thought about his heart
And how it was stitched;
Apply, apply
Needle from the cradle
Threaded to the end it reached
An extra leg just might be enough.

Assault on the senses
Later,
Later, he said,
(And I thought)
Where's Molly when you need her?
Pepper potting for me,
You've just got to remember
Only what I see
The world is mine
When it's gone, it's gone;
It's got to be red,
See?
Apply, apply,
We all need an orchestra
Before we die.

Progeny

Some awful helix
Dances on my grave
I trust
If not in God
Then in some other providence

Some fruitful bundle
From some other part
Than loins
I hope will come -
Bud the gorgeous tree of knowledge

Leave me without thought -
I have left you
For posterity
A richer vessel than my flesh, I hope
Which thought little, if at all,
Wild indeed
And only improvident
It shall bring me nonetheless blind pride.

Glass House

Give whatever you can afford
They said, so I wondered
At what point my love becomes expensive.

I look at you,
Deploring every day my suspicions
First and foremost
You may be better than me,
Worth more,
And I am determined
To put away
Naughty thoughts
Harshly sheltering under soft veils.

You are a bright day shining
On a very dark room
But it's all Other
Unless you use mirrors,
Inverse without glass

All I can think
Is
How much
Do I give away?
You're a stone's throw
Held in check

At this, my love becomes a point
So sharp and valuable it cuts rings
From the hard veil
And you will need more than gauze
To cover the round wound
Air blown and cold

Suddenly I remember
Those who do
Should not,
So nor shall I.

Grand Schemes

If I were
For the sake
Of argument
To find fame,
Would people who
Once knew more
Than my name
Come forward
And make
Gains from knowing me?

If I were
For the sake
Of this narrative
To parade
Naked indoors
With lights on
And blinds stayed
Open, wide
Awake,
Would they tell on me?

If I were
For the sake
Of old decency
To pretend
I'm sensible
And never
Will offend,
Will truth out
And make
Money out of me?

If I were
For the sake
Of my sanity
To make out
My habits are
Quite normal
And take out
The weird rich
Fruitcake,
Will they laugh at me?

In the grand scheme
No matter matters;
No one will know if the image shatters:
I am always just what I seem.